T0199039

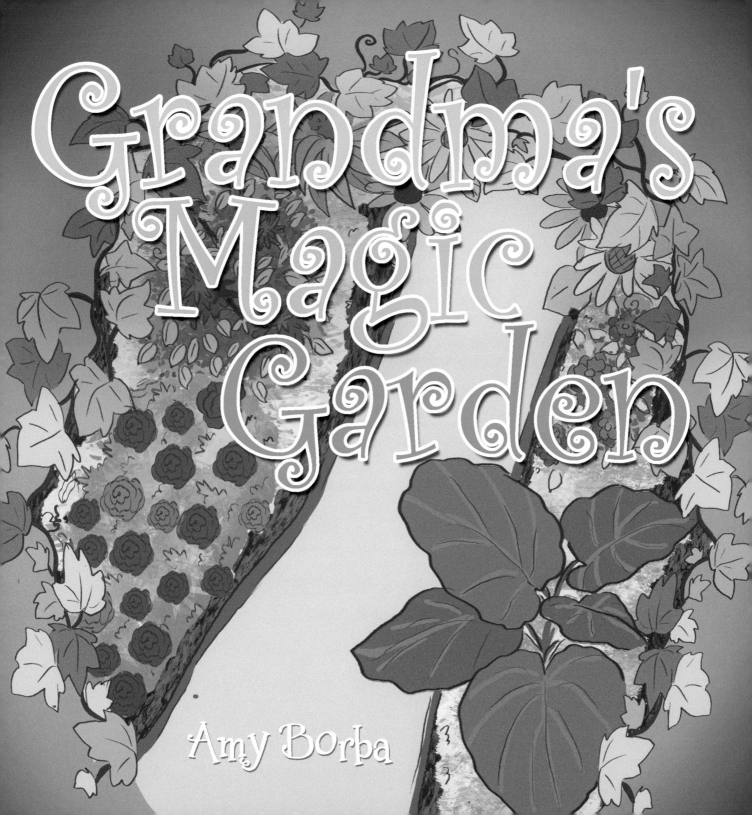

Grandma's Magic Garden

Amy Borba

To order additional copies of this book, contact:
Xlibris
844-714-8691
www.Xlibris.com
Orders@Xlibris.com

ISBN: Softcover   978-1-6641-4707-2
        Hardcover   978-1-6641-4708-9
        EBook   978-1-6641-4709-6

Print information available on the last page

Rev. date: 12/08/2020

Dedicated to my precious mom
whose love, faith and beauty
made every moment magical;
may your legacy carry on in
the pages of this book.

Early in the morning while most children sleep Justin wakes up with too much excitement to keep.

"Gavin! Wake up! We spent the night! Let's go wake up grandma, the sun is bright."

Grandma gets up with yawns and tired eyes "let's get this day started, little guys!"

She goes to get Katie, who is bouncing around her bed, "come little girl, let's get you all fed."

Sitting around the glass kitchen table she gets very quiet as if to tell a tale. She looks at us excitedly "did you hear that sound, DID you hear that sound?!" she asks repeatedly, "It's coming from the ground, it's time to go! The plants are about to grow!!"

We stuff our mouths with the last of the eggs "to the garden, Grandma" we all beg!

She slides open the door, the fresh morning breeze tickles our face, we run to the garden, little feet rattle the place! "Slow down there kiddos, no running by the pool, our work is in the garden, come see how cool!"

A winding trail, a silly smiling snail, flowers so big, bigger than a fairytale!!

"Look at the elephant ears, they're bigger than Gavin! Go pick a flower for Mommy, they're there for the grabbin'"

13

Katie runs for a tomato, so big, so red, so juicy, so sweet! Grandma giggles as the juice falls and tickles her feet!

"Look at the mums, the zinnias too! Their beauty reminds me of my love for you! They grow and grow and shine so bright, happy little flowers. My delight"

Hours go by as fast as a blink "I'm getting hungry now, it's time for lunch I think!"

Milk and bread it is, our favorite yummy treat. We sit at the table; feet cool and muddy, dirty little fingers grasp the food to fill our tummy.

Grandma stands there and stares. All her favorite little people filling up the chairs. She looks at our faces, full and done, and she rattles off her favorite saying "this is fun".

Printed in the United States
By Bookmasters